UNA WOODS was born and raised in Belfast where she now lives.
Her first published short stories, prose pieces and poems appeared in anthologies, magazines and newspaper pages in Ireland and the UK.
The Dark Hole Days, a novella and short stories, was published by Blackstaff Press in 1984.
Her play Grace Before Meals was staged by Cello Productions Theatre Company at festivals in Ireland, including Dublin Theatre FringeFest, and Earagail arts, in the early 2000's.
Afternoons is her first published selection of poems. It marks the transition to a pared landscape injected with images.

Other Una Woods books published by Ashtrees:
Still flight, words that deserted their stories, short prose pieces, 2008;
Mr and Mrs McKeown the accidental maze–
a novella or 4 short stories, 2010;
an icicle for an eye, notepoems 2011;
2 plays, Grace before meals, For want of the call, 2013;
Splintered vision, selected poems 2016;
The ordinary of the disquiet, poems, 2021.

Don't strike the moment
    so faintly
light the faint moment
    with a new match

Afternoons

by

Una Woods

First published 2006

revised 2024 Ashtrees press

All rights reserved

ISBN 978-1-8384318-9-1

Afternoons

That day the light pale skimmed slightly the
flagstones she said
This day will be the one or rather did not say if
only every day could be this day
magnified
this tiny day this shape of days
to come

She was old enough to know little. That day it
was the light was pale it skimmed slightly the
flagstones/ she moved a little on her feet.
This will do she said, this slight movement, this
faint scrape on flagstones.

There was a hint of dust, not much, a gritty feel,
underfoot the light scrunched
and above the Black mountain its suspicion
vanished/ suddenly it brightened.

Afternoons

**Peeping from her spot below she raised her
expectations to say the least
one word to a passerby
hallo**

**That day the word dulled/ only as a word on light
dulls, flattens, that day it flattened
this flat word is enough
she said
hallo
this word dulled and the little movement of feet.**

**There were a few people on the road, not many.
The shop opposite had the odd customer. In and
out/ this odd customer faint in the doorway in the
pale light then went. This dark figure in a split of
sun a glance of eye and it was gone.
This glance of eye she said
will make a figure fill a doorway seeing if I glance**

Afternoons

I see.

This pale light, this dull word, the little movement of feet. This glance of eye.

There was a shimmer of sun/ not bright a feather-torch on brick.
She turned and imagined afternoons this will do she said, for afternoons
this shimmer of sun this niggle on-
light all stops but for this afternoon I see it far on rooftops and the little breath of air.

She unravelled the rope. There was a pause. Not long/ only as a day pauses before movement before action.

This pause she said

Afternoons

will be my preparation this pause
before the rope arcs
high
before the air
whishes this imaginary pause of day.

Sounds muffled intermittently. Not to interrupt
the pause the pause was elsewhere this pause for
afternoons
sounds will do she said
in the meantime she threw the rope over her head.
It rested on the ground at her heels. She arranged
her feet precisely. These feet together stock-still
the air fidgeted along railings
a piece of sweet paper
crinkled
this crinkle and road air held.

Afternoons

Suddenly her front door opened/ a shaft of dim
hall light caught the corner of her eye a sudden
shaft of dim hall wall this wall a dim yellow
opened in
hallo
another passerby
she said
and then it was the front door closed. Without
turning she saw her father's figure on the path/
this figure with hat aslant, this tweed coat, this
shade moving in her right vision her feet stock
still
 the little crinkle trapped
on railings
on the pause for afternoons.

She lifted the rope lifted her feet together
slightly off the ground.
This will do she said
this little skipping.

Afternoons

This pale light, this dull word, the little movement of feet. This glance of eye, the pause, this crinkle, another passerby (hallo), the shadow of her father in her eye, these feet together slightly off the ground, this shape of tiny days to come.

Nothing in a book taught me how to take
the next breath
The city air comes sudden back
as a breath-story about to be told

Sunsmoke,
on the factory road beyond the dark caps of men
thumped on the light possible
words impossible   impossible to tell
the pagepale sky an open camouflage
for life

        and everything uttered is out there
            like air mumbling in unison
          its unanswered prayer

The road of dusk spun away
where I stood tidily in step with
traffic/ groaned on and off bumpers
dulled out of the sun/ I kept faith with
the bottom of a voice scraped from a
hall opened out to the deafening evening
barely ajar

give me patience

A sharp gust of shadow shook the puddle
black water widened like glass
sky at night
A face turned once the other way
A flight of stairs up to a landing
devoid of day/
light broke into the tumbling shadow

get away

The cello sound of the road in summer
the thrumming of the sun on dry brick
the twang of a butterfly in the yard
waiting for the lightness of music to return
a note in the air of possibility

The night of a silent street-lamp
vast yellow to gaze
up at the window
depths of empty
yellow if anything to fizzle on
a shining rim to dark

Duet 1

Can she go to the pictures? I said to her brother at the door.
I don't know, he said, leaning his shoulder against the wall.
Can you not find out? I said, standing straight.
What's in it for me? he said, folding his arms.
What? I said, holding my arms by my side.
You heard me, he said, crossing his foot.
What would there be? I said, twisting my foot.

Behind me the middle of the afternoon hummed away. In front of me another Saturday wasted.

What are you going to see? he said, looking me down and down.
I don't know, I said, sidling sidewards.
That's not good enough, he said.
How do you know? I said.
Have it you way, he said.
Carry on, I said, having an idea.

Duet 1 (cont.)

Is that an offer? he said, having a laugh.

What? I said.

Where do you plan to do it? he said.

Do what? I said.

Carry on, he said.

In the pictures, I said.

Right, he said, I'll get my coat.

The mist of late September
contented itself in the city lights
    lit up
sudden dim corners
glimpsed passing by
   voices vying
in a dusk shop doorway

the tin light of early October
lit on the road
then flicked on and off kerbs
like a silver skipping-rope

call me in

The city road lived on its nerves
edgy brick tensed its walls
chimneys sneaked out timid smoke
windows darted their glass in the shadows
parlours took cover behind net curtains
    a child sat upright at an upright piano
a front door jumped to the turn of a key
Beautiful Dreamer peppered the hall

                              to live on a paving stone
                              the life of inner skipping
                              narrowly missing the
                              rope

The brass neck of summer
to alarm streets out of their secret sleep
and drab them in net brick
so they have nowhere to hide

a whizz of fields lies waiting
short stops in small stations
Tandragee, Poyntz Pass, Scarva,
A hedge cut into a careful man

Breathe steadily through the slow night
if sleep comes it comes
then awake to the dream
of tomorrow's journey

From the midnight town the cathedral bell
shook the night to its dark
black time rang its worst
judas stars juked out of a bitter sky
the frightened moon forsook all space

the small gate clinked- like dropped silver
a dog in an outhouse howled three times

uneasy sleep started and fitted through the guilty hours;
slithering out of the dawn the mist-risen fields
barely believed
the bright lonely crow of the rooster

        and the light across the fields
        like a lost way
        or home in an instant

Nothing is further than here
   nothing on earth is
than this bleat of light on a street
at ten o'clock in the morning

suddenly a door opens
   as little as possible
a ray of dim shines from a morning
hall ajar with solitary

   silence is broken
   as softly as possible
a figure slips into a slit of day
then closes it behind/
   a cloud
a snib of sun goes
   click

Someone has stolen the sun
and left a trail of light
across the countryside
fields rise ransacked
hedges thrown here and there
cows tramp the soiled earth
on the broken bank of the river

a figure singled out
on the grey stone bridge
looks straight ahead
at the homeless heart of things

                    don't think there is more
                    than the shiver of grass
                    through the low field
                    on a particular summer's
                    day

the moment

we paused to catch our breath

and looked out across the yellow distance

blurred corn bright at its end;

or the enemy appeared from the white cottages

below

        voices in jagged white

        a gull yell in the clouds

        a walk on the M 1

        lifting off early tarmac

        lit black by the setting sun

Duet 2

Tell her I'm here, I said to her brother at the door.
Where? he said, straining over my head.
Here, I said, craning my neck.
I don't see anybody, he said.
Lower down, I said.
There's nobody there, he said, looking down at the ground.
A bit higher up, I said.
Oh, he said, coming on my knees by chance.
Tell her I'm here, I said.
She's not in, he said, glancing around the street.
Where is she? I said, peering up the hall.
She's out, he said, flicking back his hair.
Out where? I said, straightening my fringe.
How would I know, he said.
Who with? I said.
You, he said.
How can that be? I said.
Ask her, he said.

Duet 2 (cont.)

She's not in, I said.

Well done, he said.

Thanks, I said.

Don't mention it, he said.

Tell her I called, I said.

I won't be here, he said.

Where will you be? I said.

Nowhere you need to know, he said, taking out his comb and re-doing his quiff.

As a matter of fact, I said, turning away, I'll be somewhere else myself.

        The sudden life in the glimmer
        that hangs in a hallway
        otherwise
        lost in the space
        of a door that opens
        in

And the street like a desert at sunset
stretches, hazy with disappearing
figures like far camels
improvise with dark
lamplight like sand in the low sun
pool-shimmers on pavement
      still
silhouettes blacken against brick
      silence
shines on a slate horizon

the night city gleams
                    afar

In the door-quake of an afternoon
still-shocks tremored, a hall cracked
and a chasm of wall opened
to the silence of a deserted road-   small wonder
life after shuddered with survival
and the sun-crumbled buildings
    stood like statues
        rescued from a former religion

An empty chair in an attic waiting to be vacated
a noteless piano in a parlour at the dusk of play
a woman whiles at her entry door, revealing
the inner grey   somewhere
    a nameless voice calls out a voiceless name

these knife-questions blunt like wings on cement

The city road is smithereened
    shards of sunset cut deep/
shadows bandage; out of the injured evening
a figure limps
dripping in glow

night closes over
the waiting wound

a helicopter haunts the blue, rocks
the round of peace
it goes; an uneasy sky is stretched
to breaking

beneath the icy clouds, a man
is drilling a hole

There was a calm thud of open/
air landed on the road like a rope wound round
and round the earth/ took an instant to recover its spell/
bound for future days
I heard singing from a street close by
A light went on in an attic window

A black taxi in another town
might well break down the barriers
made of air-
tight days we rushed towards the train/
  squealed to a stop
in the G N R

All change at Goraghwood

The future is late tonight
the particular bang of a front door

the night is angry with the day
the white howl of a dog at midnight

the trees are shooting at the stars
the fire of branch on a lamp-lit blind

the void is shaken in its space
the grip of rubber soles in a hall

the child is awake and staring
the future is here tonight

Streets made sense of city life;
doors, down to earth opened
and closed;
footsteps paid tribute to halls that had
no illusions;
parlours held private conversations that promised
to go no further   imperceptibly
through net curtains dusk deemed it necessary
    to glimmer and gradual
street-lamps to unsettle the everyday

                    there are sounds that
                            stop
                    all thought of moving
                            on
                    and silences

Stars ice-pin the sky
trees everest the orchard
in the back white-washed yard
the handle of the pump sticks fast
a dog's bark buries the countryside
    deep in muffled white
    the future is remembered
Grandmother stands at the back door
holding the big iron kettle in her hand

we will turn in the dazed dazzle
and laughed at the very idea
of water

May the 11th

>Polyanthus made mischief
>on the landing windowsill
>tricksy light dimpled
>through glass
>
>then quick stepless silence
>the slight raise of her eyebrows
>Oh, you're there-

Time called time on time
while clocks ticked crazily on
timing the speed of void

or

Meticulous time
chooses its moment to say
nothing changes
but the day

The mauve melody of the hydrangea
steps recede on stones
like a drummer walking away
still beating ever fainter
up the path towards the hydrangea

the moment spreads
like thinly-stopped time
the horizon has no hope of holding

finding feebleness
in the first Autumn flutterings
as if the very act of falling
could fail mid-air

since to be present is not
    possible
and to be possible is not
    present
the past and future fable
the present-possible

Nowhere more present
nowhere more frail
than the daygone by
the faintsome air on that sea front

nowhere more past
nowhere more real
than the skyby width
the lightsome fade on this city horizon

                    the single sun-slant
                    rescued place
                    from where it
                    coldly
                    shone
                    now place-lit
                    it belongs

Imagine
sitting in a train travelling in the reflected
approval
of the wide window
leaning on the rhythm of the moving carriage
like a child rocked in the unawares
of departure or arrival

conjuring up cows on a hill

The wood pigeon is urgent in the evening
the longest day is quickly close
the sun tunnels out of a clear sky
like a prisoner on solitary parole

April has no sharp corners
it sits like a flimsy net on the city's afternoon
frail-flits on houses like limp loss

it bites at cloudy memory
with bland teeth
till a milky sun seeps through

light skims the top
of other Aprils

                              in the Spring still
                              in the afternoon
                              the squeak of a swing
                              rips the big yard's
                              summer

When the hum-song of voices
in the summer kitchen
lilted the highs and lows-
the time it takes to pause in this present silence-
outside the door with the jingling handle

a chit of wing
against a china sky
blue voices swum in time-nets
a flutter of cows in a flute of hill

    the hum of a fridge
    like inside day

Carlingford 1999

not a sound around

sshhh

listen

Talofa lava lau Susuga, Leone

Sea, sand and sky
Samoa, St Croix
your odyssean heart a far cry
from this staid street; stories like bright ships
travel, or golden suns threaded through a city
letterbox
the yellow bird plumbs through the still air
sugar sparkles on hall tiles unpecked

from this watered-down window on your horizon
waves break through fir trees in small needles of
light. And can't know openly the sea.
A deep southern day dwindles to a northerly
notion of twilight. Slits of pink suggest a sun.

all at once a far cry
ebbs into these worlds apart
and there is nothing in the room but sea, sand and
sky to mark the leaving

More than this winter sky
time whitens

stops short of width or a way
to make it matter

white fields
a blackbird jittering in a frozen yard

only that it is winter in the suburbs
now

now
silence stops short on glass
and white as a moment matters

                        Try to make a moment of it
                        a day is too great a loss
                              to bear

The breathless air, birdless bird-song
where is what is happening
between winter and spring
seasonless afternoons fail to fall fully
and eveningless nights drop like stone shadows

where what is happening is
before and after

breakable shaves of browny-
gold sunslit the afternoon air
fine needles of yellow
prick gently aslant a bus/
rumbles through the narrow eye
of Autumn

There's nothing to say what day
this Sunday is- the drone of grey sits
like Sundays rolled into one
unexceptional day; the quiet is as dutiful
as the click of heels on a pavement
chapel bound, or a family in line forced out
for the Sunday afternoon walk
    the light is in a rut
        like the prospect of park railings

what indifference a day makes

        houses pressed in a perpetual row
        walls raised like rites of standing
        muffling up towards the mountain
        traffic
        like a whispered prayer for movement

A door ajars to a jolt of road
a house aslants to a hesitant world
half-open the afternoon
is finding its feet
on a threshold of home
sensing the child is standing on the brink
                                          of birth

        it was never revealed
        what the sudden certainty hoped to
        be
        nor when

Ha-ha
the hardly happening is hovering
   the where is what
   is whetting the when
a bird is blasting a berry
on a bedraggled branch

far far
faint flagstone pigeon
butting the breaking ground

Stark twig-tree
against the peach-pale sky; time
    slits through the broken
  years. It is four o'clock on a winter afternoon
and
      your awkward branches cut out the in-
   between leaving extremes of moment
      bare yet unbroken

Like the clatter of a town clock
the bright moon strikes the sky
and everywhere rings out
like those clear hills around
the cathedral

The metallic music of a hammer
is exactly how it was meant to be
outside the entry door
of a yard where the clang came close
to celebrating the deadened city spell

When a place opens and closes
in a dove's stark call
in a dove's muffled coo
today is yesterday's tomorrow
today

A thrush is flittering
on inklings of snow
its frail pecking makes no impression
on the frozen ground

close-by a magpie is prizing
a stolen crumb
carefully parading it from branch
to comfortless branch

sometimes void has
a homely ring
like knowing night from the inside

or standing in the doorway
    of its echo

in the carefully constructed space
of a street lamp
that renounces all other
life

                        and the grey candle burns
                        in the mid-afternoon

Summer has too much day
going for it, gleams that start
on street corners and bite at night
are more at home with high
expectations-
though the swallow's narrow flight
through a slit of hay-loft window
brings swift
consolation

The slow glisten of an evening
a star rustles leaf-like   the road is silent
as a winter forest
laden and sparkling   a voice breaks
like a lone stick, sharp and stopped
under a full skyless moon

As if it could mean
life lived
in the expanse of a moment
like a train stopping
full-speed ahead

and here come the corn-fields
quick! here come the corn-fields

Here is the cows' byre   brimming in sunlight
in the busy yard
    or is it life
squatting in the bright idea
of a simple doorway

Don't confuse the hub-bub
of the afternoon road
with a place to live

a lorry is a breath
of fresh rumble
or the air itself
is getting ready
to tremble

the gate scraping over
the dirt-stones in the big yard
has everything to answer for

Today there's a splintering
at the height of things, a fine
clashing of shades in the fullness
of disintegration, a brilliant
         breaking up
of patch-lit places-   the past's future
is parting into fragile shape

     and here's the orchard   bunching up
     in August behind the sun-yard
        or is it hope
     hiding in the rosy thought
     of an apple falling

A dog stopped barking somewhere
    listen-
if you dare

The front door opened
    and closed
like a future given
    and taken

the bright wheeze of a bus
to a scheduled stop

The pier road
stones stooped down
to the black water's edge
slurping at night

the lights along the far bay
turned on in time
back in time
just in time

in the scattered city leaves
it seemed steps had found their exact fall

and words caught at breezy corners
had the crisp air of the precisely said

The road-works are silent
suggesting life was but a passing
clamour
come to think of it
the silence starts to quake
on another road
suggesting sound is all
in the mind

        by some slight chance
        things shifted into their
              otherness
        and arrived back where they
        were
              otherwise
        slightly themselves

and here's the garden   fragrant
with figures in summer dress
    or is it the future
faking under the full bloom
of fragile flowers

pebbles are making silence
on the white sun front
unbeknownst to sound width waits
for the crunch to come

                to belong to a
                  moment
            of Friday 5 o'clock

A piano in a parlour
is the sound of sorrow
but for the black notes
and the white

everything has its immediate other
or it itself
      is vast

    there's a joyful corner of a room
        where dust sparkles
        and no-one knows
        you live there

There's brittle summer
in this blue winter sky
there are folds of fields
shifting away in an iceberg haze

on a frost-roofed horizon
the shallow river crunches
over sun-white stones

so long as winter has memory
and memory has narrowed eyes

       the way light broke on a bus
       flashed on a silver wheel

       and there was light

A thump of play
on a gable wall; the sun slaps
day hard; voices
trap distance
like a careworn future
embarked on in the afternoon

The hatsome days
a slant of rim on a road
              of greetings
              tweed sound
all around; jaunty settings-out
then
the hatless hours-
faded tip of light to
battered night returns

The words used
are words exiled
from their source- as then
exiled from home, from street
the smoky twilight tinkered with the barren
loneness
and the idea took root that something beyond
being there
shone

don't say it's not the twilight
alone

                houses in the desultory dusk
                    fail slowly
                    becoming more sure
                    of time

Is there something in the cold north air
that is where
    we are

barely standing
    exposed
as icicles saved by a winter sun

seagulls on city roofs prove
    the point
as if slate could be
a north-lit sea
and this is where we
    belong

    the blue patience of a sky
    rewarded by the suddenness
        of a day

the hammering in the street has stopped
exactly

but the job is unfinished
and the air is full of it

                there's a certain light
                that has a memory all its own
                its secret about to be made
                            known

the shiver of evening
on the empty street

like things on the pin-point
of happening

sea, fields and streets
a trinity of landscapes
one on a clear day
believed as once
    seen

        the warm gravel
        under the wheel that stops
        outside the gate

the electric light shining
on the empty bus-stop

On a Sunday the wheelbarrow
sitting in the middle of the big yard
was an idle reminder
that life depended on a week-day

                    and the small stones outside the gate
                    crunchless in the Sunday sun

the chatter of sunlight
on a linen tablecloth-
    this is real life
smoothed out
    for tea

Where a blackbird unworms
the cold soil
firing shiverings of earth
from side to side
single-searching and sifting
and untroubled by sky
and song and tree

where a blackbird digging
is free

something as simple as the robin
flitting back
and back to the same thin branch
for food

The stilted row of houses
cemented in straight sunlight
dislocated from the sun's shining
rays; there in the heart of the city
out in the cold

      the chimney pot its ordered smudge
      against the crackling sky-
      down below the fire
      is not lit

              each sound has its own life
              of silence- acutely lived

there is no point but to be
at the diminishing sound
of an aeroplane, immediately there
at the high point of fade

the yellow sun foraging
on a haystack in Connolly's field
    busily search-lighting
its future fire

    the road-drill shudders
    through hard times
    tar sun-scorched comes up
    smelling of smothered summers

Close-in
of a grey day
the soft slit of tyres through rain
like a knife through an unreached thought;
suddenly the sky clears above rooftops

to a delft-cool blue
a bird's tinny whistle
repeats the thought
cutting it dangerously thin

        always one is bettering
        the way to say
        there is more to space
        than meets the empty

How strange the unseen hour
that strikes above the emerging lamp-light
blue-grey the sky
is folding away
the past's close-kept
colour

The brown sting on an evening table
the white pang of a cup on a saucer
lulled between talk the rock-bottom of sound
words themselves red silences dropped
on a bare tiled floor forever

Come to delight in a quick thing
come to suspend the rush of standing
on a vaporous road
where traffic thrills
at a remove

        the teem of sunset
        on white paintwork
        like the harum-skarum of silence

the sudden browny dusk
like a light-hearted future
looked into

        the bang of an inner door
        without dull care

It comes back to the white square
and walking limbo-light through its cement soul
after confession

the place is lost
but its destination is just
as far away

        if the invisible can't be seen
           nothing is there
           and the wind is vacant
           in the evergreens

the sun is too close
to the page
words have no business
being shone on

        single close sounds
        are thumps on the chest
        of silence

        distant murmurings are miracles
        that can't be proved

nothing can be said that means
the pin-prick distance of a place
that had no name
beyond the Hilltown hills

I thought I had arrived
at some permanent edge
of sea-stones, and that wherever I was
I would have that possibility

now wherever I am is not the arrival
but the possibility still exists

and it comes with the clarity of the white stones
cracking on the sea-hard waves: the thought
revealed
that permanence existed out there
and I am on the edge of it

        to sense the vast
        is to know the narrow
        nothing else
        is worth the wait

in the pale sun-low net
of late August
the light is caught less needy
of the open space

        to dig with an invisible spade
        impressions out of the silence
        preparing the air
        for unspoken pleasures
        built on a tremor
            of tomorrow

        the wide blue sky
        sings with the imagination
        for all seasons

and the unseen sun is high and low

It could be that

silence dances

with sound

or that

light taps

on air

or it could be

leaves listen

in vain

    the edge of the roof is sitting well

        in the city today

a sunlit gable
like a slab of eternity
excommunicated from summer

and the street in June
was just the beginning

                              the way distance thins
                              invisible time heard
                              the faint dog-bark
                              like one thing
                                      happened

finely humming
tuned like a tree
timed to go solo
at the drop of light

Through the birch-leaves
a street-light shines
like a mistimed nest
or a city out of song
with the silver trees

    and there is nothing
    to say but what almost
    is today
    silence is sorely present
    without its other half

the black fir
against the fading sky
this scene is all
    but lost

Like a lighthouse
on an unsettled sea
memory blinks

out of the mist
a life-boat disappears

all are saved
going down

a dove on a fir branch
a pigeon on city cement
each as far away on the day

cooing and clucking

the out of surroundings shiver
of twilit tarmac
down to the corner
of the country road

the strict shadow
of a signpost
fading two ways

        the loft ticked with heat
        hay smothered its breath in bails
        footsteps on the ladder suspected
            the secret height
                of summer

A step in the evening street
is the fundamental space
for walking
away

  go the whole hog and say
  a shout from an unseen street
  suspended all belief
  leaving the shout to face
  the future alone

The faint yellow of a fanlight
like a long welcome home

something in a candle
lit room
a pin-drop of life

from the outside
flickering on a dark window
a figure shadow-waxes across a
deeply absent room
in a moment of breath-becoming
                      apparition

the place in fact, from the inside
is a city parlour, dimly lit
and the figure is holding fast
                    to a candle flame
                    for dear life

 the constancy of the made-up moment
   a way of life
   at the front door

 the glint of a brass door-knocker
 inviting the world in

 this place reached
 by means of no destination
   coming or going

www.ingramcontent.com/pod-product-compliance
Lightning Source LLC
Chambersburg PA
CBHW071734040426
42446CB00012B/2359